THE TWELVE DISCIPLES

Neville Stephens

ISBN: 978-1-78364-388-2

www.obt.org.uk

****

The Open Bible Trust

Fordland Mount, Upper Basildon, Reading, RG8 8LU, UK.

CONTENTS

Page

THE TWELVE
DISCIPLES

	Matt. 10:2-4	Mark 3:16-19	Luke 6:14-16	Acts 1:13
1	Peter	Peter	Peter	Peter
2	Andrew	James	Andrew	John
3	James	John	James	James
4	John	Andrew	John	Andrew
5	Philip	Philip	Philip	Philip
6	Bartholomew	Bartholomew	Bartholomew	Thomas
7	Thomas	Matthew	Matthew	Bartholomew
8	Matthew	Thomas	Thomas	Matthew
9	James the son of Alphaeus	James the son of Alphaeus	James the son of Alphaeus	James the son of Alphaeus
10	Thaddaeus	Thaddaeus	Simon the Zealot	Simon the Zealot
11	Simon the Zealot	Simon the Zealot	Judas son of James	Judas son of James
12	Judas Iscariot	Judas Iscariot	Judas Iscariot	–

INTRODUCTION

INTRODUCTION

In this booklet we are going to consider thirteen men, yet it is entitled *The Twelve Disciples!* The New Testament informs us that twelve apostles are to sit on twelve thrones, judging the twelve tribes of Israel (Matt. 19:28; Luke 22:30; Rev. 21:12-14). So when Judas Iscariot betrayed the Lord Jesus Christ and followed this by committing suicide, he was replaced by Matthias (Acts 1), as the Psalmist had prophesied, "may another take his place of leadership" (Acts 1:20 NIV).

Does this mean we should ignore Judas in a study dealing with the twelve disciples? We cannot. He was clearly chosen by the Lord (John 6:70; 13:18), but some will ask whether Judas was a saved person. Others ask whether he lost his salvation, if such a thing were possible. Perhaps he lost his reward of being one of the twelve who were to sit on those twelve special thrones. This is a most controversial subject, one we will consider later in this booklet.

There are four lists of the twelve disciples in the New Testament, and the name of Judas Iscariot appears in three of them, whereas Matthias is never included in any list of the twelve. In fact, Matthias is never mentioned again by name in the Bible after the selection recorded in Acts 1:23-26. The four lists as they appear in the *New International Version* are on the preceding page.

Before proceeding, we must solve some confusion that exists over the identification of certain of these disciples.

A) The Authorized Version speaks of Judas in Luke and Acts as "the brother of James", which is incorrect. The words "the brother" are in italics which indicate that they form no part of the Greek manuscripts. It simply reads "Judas of James" which is a common Greek idiom, and invariably means "son of", as in the genealogy in Luke 3:23-38. The Revised Version, and all subsequent translations, have it as "Judas the son of James" as it should be. This Judas also possessed two other names. They were

"Lebbaeus, whose surname was Thaddaeus" (Matt. 10:3 A.V.), and just "Thaddaeus" (Mark 3:18). These names were not unusual, however, for we read of Joseph Barsabbas Justus (Acts 1:23). Perhaps he began to omit the name of Judas when it became associated with a name of shame. We can only speculate, but his full name was Judas Lebbaeus Thaddaeus. In John 14:22 he is referred to as "Judas, not Iscariot" to differentiate him from the betrayer.

B) All modern translations refer to Simon as "the Zealot" which is correct, whereas the A.V. switches from "the Zealot" in Luke and Acts to "the Canaanite" in Matthew and Mark. Both cannot be true. The Greek "Zelotes" in Luke and Acts prove that Simon was a zealot. The best manuscripts for the other two references show the word to be *Kananaios* meaning *Cananaean,* not *Kananites* which means *Canaanite.* The Aramaic word for a zealot is *Cananaean,* confirming the fact that Simon was a Jewish nationalist, a patriot, not Canaanite foreigner.

C) Nathanael is one of the twelve (John 1:43-51; 21:2), yet his name does not appear in any of the four lists of the apostles. This is because he is always referred to in them by his distinguishing second name of Bartholomew. *Bar* means *son of*, therefore his complete name would be Nathanael son of Tolmai. Another clue confirming that Nathanael and Bartholomew is one and the same person is found in his great friendship with Philip. It is Philip who brings Nathanael to the Lord (John 1:43-51), and Matthew, Mark and Luke are all inspired to link Philip and Bartholomew together in their lists of the twelve.

CHAPTER ONE
PETER

CHAPTER ONE
PETER

Peter was, without any doubt, the leader of the twelve apostles. The Holy Spirit places him at the head of the four lists of the disciples to confirm his leadership, and he stands out as the spokesman of the group on many occasions. It was Peter who asked the meaning of a difficult saying (Matt. 18:21), and who enquired what was to be the reward of those who had left all to follow the Lord (Matt. 19:27).

It was Peter who asked about the fig-tree which had withered away (Mark 11:21), and about the meaning of thins which Christ had said about the end of the age (Mark 13:3). It was to Peter the Jews came asking whether the Lord had paid His taxes (Matt. 17:24), and it was Peter who answered when Christ asked who had touched Him in the crowd (Luke 8:45). It was also Peter who asked questions of the Risen Christ (John 21:20-22).

Peter, then, was regarded as the leader and together with James and John formed an inner circle of three which the Lord selected to witness some sacred moments. They were with Christ when He brought Jairus' daughter back to life (Mark 5:37; Luke 8:51); they were allowed to witness the Lord's transfiguration in glory (Matt. 17:1; Mark 9:2; Luke 9:28); they were with the Lord during His last moments in the Garden of Gethsemane (Matt. 26:37; Mark 14:33). It was Peter and John who were sent on ahead to prepare for the last Passover (Luke 22:8).

Peter's full name was Simon Peter, and on many occasions he is referred to in this way, or simply as "Peter" or "Simon". Twice he is called Symeon (Acts 15:14; 2 Peter 1:1) which is the Hebrew name, Simon being the Gentile modification. He is also referred to as Cephas on several occasions, Cephas being the Aramaic and Peter being the Greek for a rock, the name given him by the Lord (Matt. 16:16-18).

He was a fisherman by trade, and it was from the boats that Christ called him to become a fisher of men (Mark 1:16-17). Notice the immediate reaction of Peter and his brother Andrew in leaving their livelihood to follow this Galilean preacher (v18), such must have been the irresistible nature of Christ. He was a married man (1 Cor. 9:5). His home was in Capernaum, and it may well be that Peter's house was the Lord's headquarters when He was in Capernaum, for it was there that He healed Peter's mother-in-law (Mark 1:29-30; Luke 4:38-39).

Peter was probably the first of the twelve to recognize who Jesus of Nazareth really was. At Caesarea Philippi the Lord asked the twelve, "Whom do men say that I the Son of Man am?" The reply varied from John the Baptist to Elijah, from Jeremiah to one of the other prophets. When Christ asked *them* who they thought He was, it was Peter who boldly exclaimed, "Thou art the Christ, the Son of the living God" (Matt. 16:13-16).

It was following on from this that the Lord made the great statement to Peter that on this rock He would build His church. The rock, surely, was

Peter's confession of faith, a confession which is needed by every person who turns from darkness to light and true belief in the saving grace of the Lord Jesus Christ.

No sooner had Peter made his great declaration of faith, however, than he followed it with one of his greatest mistakes which earned a stern rebuke from the Lord. From this time, Christ began to tell the disciples about His forthcoming death and resurrection, yet Peter seems to lose sight of the glory of the latter and concentrate on the horror of the death of his Master. In his ignorance, he actually begins to rebuke the Lord, claiming "this shall not be unto thee" (Matt. 16:22).

The Lord's reply in the following verse is quite astonishing, "Get thee behind Me *Satan:* thou art an offence to Me". The spirit of anti-Christ can enter even the greatest of God's servants, and here Peter allows Satan to ruin his testimony of the previous verses. As we know, Judas went even further, for the devil actually entered him (Luke 22:3). Peter's reaction was very natural of course, and borne out of love and devotion for his Master, yet nevertheless this was the spirit of anti-Christ and completely alien to the goal for which Christ had come to earth (John 12:27), hence the violent response of the Lord Jesus.

An even blacker time lay in store for Peter, for shortly he was to deny his Master three times. He displayed his impulsive nature once again by affirming unbreakable loyalty to the Lord in the upper room (Matt. 26:33-35), and by striking off the high priest's servant's ear when the arrest took place in Gethsemane, once again exhibited a witness which was anti-Christian – as is clearly evidenced by the words of the Lord (John 18:10-11). But in the courtyard of the high priest's house, his faith weakened when he was recognized and he ended up denying that he even knew Jesus of Nazareth, just as the Lord had predicted (Matt. 26:69-75; Mark 14:66-72; Luke 22:54-62; John 18:15-27).

However, it is very easy for us to cast stones from the comfort of our armchairs, and certain points have to be noted. Peter, at least, was in the courtyard of the high priest when the other disciples had long since fled, and his failure was the kind of failure that could only have happened to a brave, loyal man. He alone of the twelve was in a position to fail having ventured into enemy territory out of love and loyalty. He was the only one of the twelve there and we should not let his failure cloud his bravery.

It was Peter who stepped out in faith and beckoned the Lord to call him on to the water when the other disciples sat back in terror in the wave-lashed boat. He recognized his Lord while the others doubted. He had the unique experience of walking on water and although he wavered once again, when he took his eyes off the Lord, he was once more the only one in that position (Matt. 14:24-31). Yes, Peter was impulsive and impetuous and he made mistakes, but he was never afraid to venture forth and his motives were always correct.

Peter recovered from his traumatic experience in denying the Lord, and is found with the other disciples on the resurrection morning. The angel at the tomb sent a special message to Peter (Mark

16:7), and it was Peter and John who were the first of the apostles to visit the tomb (John 20:2-6). It was to Peter that the Lord made a special resurrection appearance (1 Cor. 15:5).

When we pass from the gospels to the Acts, Peter is still very much to the forefront. It was he who made the first move to choose another apostle to replace Judas (Acts 1:15); it was Peter who was the spokesman on the day of Pentecost and who made the first speech after the Lord's ascension (Acts 2:14-40); it was Peter, who, with John, healed the lame man at the beautiful gate of the temple (Acts 3:1-11); it was Peter who defied the Sanhedrin when he and John were arrested for preaching Christ (Acts 4:1-22); 12:1-11); it was Peter who went to Samaria when the gospel was first preached there, and who dealt with the deceit of Simon Magus (Acts 8:12-25); it was Peter who dealt grimly with the duplicity of Ananias and Sapphira (Acts 5:1-11); and it was Peter who healed Aeneas and Dorcas (Acts 9:32-43).

But the greatest step that Peter took during the Acts was to receive the Gentile Cornelius into the fellowship of believers (Acts 10:1-11:18). It is often overlooked that Cornelius was the first Gentile to whom the message of the Lord Jesus was preached in Acts. The Jews were the chosen people and they despised the Gentiles. But the Lord chose Peter to be the vessel to start the universal spread of the gospel of Jesus Christ, and at the Council of Jerusalem it was Peter who was instrumental in opening the door further for the Gentiles (Acts 15:7-11).

During the gospel period, Peter and the others had been clearly instructed, "Go not into the way of the Gentiles, and into any city of the Samaritans enter ye not. But go rather to the lost sheep of the house of Israel" (Matt. 10:5-6). The Lord Himself endorsed this later when He proclaimed that He "was not sent but unto the lost sheep of the house of Israel" (Matt. 15:24). Israel was very much to the fore during the Gospels and the Acts, thus Peter acted courageously when he went to Cornelius.

After the Council of Jerusalem at Acts 15, Peter passes from the pages of the New Testament (with the exception of his two epistles). Very little else is known of this great man of God. Tradition has it that he was crucified upside down for his faith, for he considered himself unworthy to die in the same manner as his Lord. Impulsive. Impetuous. Impatient. Yes, Peter was all of these. But he was also a great man of faith, love, loyalty, actions and trustworthiness – the true leader amongst the twelve.

CHAPTER TWO
JAMES AND
JOHN

CHAPTER TWO

JAMES AND JOHN

James and John were the sons of Zebedee and along with Peter formed the nucleus of leadership among the apostles. They were privileged to be with the Lord on several intimate occasions as we have already seen.

They were fishermen by trade, and were in partnership with the other pair of brothers, Peter and Andrew (cp. Luke 5:10 with Matt. 4:18-20). They were very close, for the three synoptic gospels nearly always pair the two together. James, in fact, is never mentioned in the Bible without John except at his death. We know more of John, for he seems to take a more prominent role and is often depicted as second only to Peter in the group.

It appears that James and John were of a violent disposition on occasions, and the Lord even called them "Boanerges, the sons of thunder" (Mark 3:17). This is best illustrated by the account in Luke when the brothers wanted to bring fire down from heaven on the people of a Samaritan village for not receiving the Lord (9:51-56), an amazing reaction after spending considerable time in the presence of the Prince of Peace! John also wanted to stop a man who had been casting out demons in the Lord's name (Luke 9:49).

James and John also appear to emerge as men of ambition. They desired the best position in the kingdom, incurring the displeasure of the other ten disciples (Mark 10:35-45). Their motive was in all probability pure, wanting to serve the Lord faithfully and thus qualify for the positions at the right hand and left hand of Christ in glory, but the other ten were not impressed and some commentators view this as worldly ambition. If there was any purely human motive attached to this request, it was possibly on the part of their mother. She, quite naturally, wanted the best for her sons and Matthew accredits this proposal to the mother of James and John (Matt. 20:20-28).

In his gospel, describing himself as the "disciple Jesus loved", John records several events that happened to him apart from his brother James. It was to his care that the Lord entrusted Mary His mother on the Cross (John 19:26-27); it was the beloved disciple who arrived first at the tomb on the resurrection morning (John 20:1-10); it was the future of John which Peter enquired about at a post-resurrection dinner (John 21:20-21).

When we move to the Acts period we still find John in a very prominent role, but he never speaks in the events recorded for us, for Peter is always the spokesman. He now seems to emerge as a constant companion of Peter, but what of James? He disappears from the scene because he had been given the privilege of becoming the first of the twelve disciples to suffer martyrdom, and event described for us by Luke, "Now about that time Herod the king stretched forth his hands to vex certain of the church. And he killed James the brother of John with the sword" (Acts 12:1-2). This is the only occasion in the New Testament where James appears without his brother, and even then John's name is mentioned.

James, then, lived as one of the inner circle of three and died a martyr's death, yet very little else is known of this disciple. It appears he was content to play a lesser role, living in the shadow of his younger brother. This illustrates humility and a lack of jealousy and we can safely guess that James possessed these qualities along with his great faith and love.

John, however, continued to serve his risen Lord and is seen with Peter at the beautiful gate (Acts 3:1-10); before the Sanhedrin (Acts 4:1-22); in Samaria (Acts 8:14); and is named as one of the pillars of the Jerusalem church together with James (the Lord's brother) and Peter (Gal. 2:9). Although he was not a spokesman like Peter, he was a leader and it is commonly believed that he was the inspired channel used of God to write the gospel and the three epistles which bear his name together with the book of Revelation.

Some traditions have it that John did not suffer martyrdom, but died of old age in Ephesus. Scripture does not include his death. It does offer a clue, however. Returning to Mark 10, the Lord told both James and John that they would "indeed drink of the cup that I drink of; and with the baptism that I am baptized withal shall ye be baptized" (v 39). In the context of this passage, the Lord is clearly referring to His cup of suffering and baptism of death. These two brothers were to suffer in the same way. James was executed by Herod as we have already seen. John's death is not recorded in the New Testament, but there are traditions of a martyr's death for John[1], as well as of a quiet end at Ephesus. We cannot be sure either way, but Mark 10:39 would appear to endorse the former, thus ending the life of the apostle whom the Lord loved.

---

[1] For more on the evidence of a martyr's death for John, see *John: His life and writings* or Appendix 2 of *Approaching the Bible,* both by Michael Penny, published by the Open Bible Trust and both are available as eBooks from Amazon and Apple and as a KDP paperback from Amazon..

CHAPTER THREE ANDREW

CHAPTER THREE
ANDREW

The last of this quartet of brothers and partners in the fishing business is Andrew. Although not one of the inner circle of three, he must have been on the fringe of it for his name always appears in the first four in the lists of disciples, as we saw in the introduction to this booklet, and in Matthew's and Luke's narratives he is placed second only to his brother Peter. There was also one occasion in the gospels where he was linked with the other three in a leading role, when the four of them asked the Lord privately what would be the signs of the end of the age (Mark 13:1-4).

Andrew, like James, lived in the shadow of his more illustrious brother, apparently without resentment. Just as James appears to have accepted the situation in a gracious manner, so it seems to apply to Andrew. Scripture never records any personal animosity between these two sets of brothers.

Andrew was from Bethsaida, as was Peter (John 1:44), and he started off as a follower of John the Baptist, along with another disciple who was probably John. It appears from John's account that Andrew was the first of the twelve to attach himself to the Lord Jesus, soon to be followed by his brother (John 1:35-42). Bethsaida was nearly 100 miles from Bethany (where John was preaching) up in the north east of the country. Therefore he was obviously prepared to travel long and far to find the truth, first from John the Baptist and then from the person Who was *the Truth*.

With the exception of the above event quoted from Mark 13, the only time Andrew appears in the synoptic gospels is in the lists of the twelve, and at his calling by the Lord Jesus. When we move on to the fourth gospel, we find three accounts of actions by Andrew and in each case it is him bringing someone to see the Messiah. It is almost as if Andrew had no doubts from the start, and was delighted to bring people to show them a way out of their darkness.

First of all Andrew had no hesitation in following Christ when the Baptist pointed out to him "Behold the Lamb of God". He had no doubts. He followed, and very quickly afterwards he was bringing Peter to Him, for he was convinced "We have found the Messiah" (John 1:36-41). Remember it is Andrew who brings Peter to the Lord, yet afterwards he is quite content to take a back seat and allow his brother to play the dominant role.

The second account in John has Andrew bringing the boy with the five loaves and two fishes to Christ prior to the feeding of the 5000 (John 6:8-9). The third event is even more significant, for some Greeks came to worship the Lord at one of the Jewish feasts, and Philip was not quite sure what to do. He explains the situation to Andrew who has no doubts. Gentile or no Gentile, they must see the Lord (John 12:20-22). Andrew seems to be a natural missionary. There is only one Person who can solve the problems of the world today, and it was the same nearly 2000 years ago when He walked the plains of Palestine. Andrew was aware of this, therefore his answer was very simple – take them to see the One who could show them true light and happiness. This is the first account we have in the New Testament of Gentiles seeking the Lord. They may have been proselytes, but it is also quite possible that they were non-Jews who would be allowed to worship in the outer courts of the temple. All we do know is that Andrew was clear in his mind that the Lord Jesus Christ could save every person, whether Jew or Gentile, and in doing so he showed the way to his brother who was later to be instrumental in the salvation of the first Gentile recorded in Scripture, Cornelius, as we have already seen.

CHAPTER FOUR
THE MIDDLE
GROUP OF
FOUR

CHAPTER FOUR
THE MIDDLE GROUP
OF FOUR

The four lists of the apostolic band seem to fit nicely into three quartets. The first group, as we have seen, is quite an obvious foursome, being generally considered as the leading four, all being partners in the fishing trade, and being two sets of brothers.

The next four are not quite so obvious, yet the Holy Spirit inspired the evangelists to group them together in all four lists although the order does alter. Philip is always fifth; Bartholomew is sixth on three occasions; Matthew and Thomas seem to switch positions a great deal. The three quartets all start with the same leader, namely Peter for group one, Philip for group two, and James the son of Alphaeus for the third group.

A) PHILIP

All that we really know about Philip is contained in the Gospel of John, for Matthew, Mark and Luke only refer to him in their lists of the twelve. Even his one reference in Acts is merely a mention of his name in verse thirteen of the opening chapter.

We must not confuse the apostle Philip with the evangelist who was one of the seven chosen to serve tables (Acts 6:1-5), and who featured in the marvelous preaching campaign in Samaria and who was instrumental in the conversion of the Ethiopian eunuch (Acts 8:5-40). The clue to the differentiation lies in verses 14-18 where Peter and John were sent to Samaria to lay hands on the believers so that they could receive the Holy Ghost, for this gift was only passed on by an apostle. If this Philip had been the apostle, there would have been no need to send Peter and John.

Philip makes four appearances in John's gospel from which we can glean a few small glimpses into his character, for very little is actually written of this apostle. He came from Bethsaida, the same town as Peter and Andrew so there is a possibility that he too was a fisherman although it is not recorded. His first action after seeing the Messiah was to go and inform his friend Nathanael, thus displaying a missionary tendency, a requirement that the Lord sought in all of the twelve if they were to become fishers of men. Nathanael was skeptical, but Philip refused to be drawn into an argument or to be beaten. He merely retorted "Come and see" (John 1:43-46), for he knew that seeing was believing.

The next time we meet Philip is at the feeding of the 5000, for it is to Philip that Christ addresses the question about feeding such a large crowd (John 6:5-7), showing that he had some sort of position of responsibility in the group. Yet in the account of the Greeks wanting to see the Lord in John 12:20-22, Philip seems to shirk the responsibility as we have already seen, and passes the authority to Andrew. He had some qualities of leadership, but not enough to be included in the first four, hence his probable placing of the fifth in all four listings.

The last reference to Philip in the New Testament is not a happy one, for the Lord upbraids him for his unbelief (John 14:8-9). This happened in the upper room at the Passover supper. The Lord had just called Himself "The Way, The Truth and The Life" yet Philip misses the point and requests to see the Father. Philip knew that the Lord was a special person, probably the Messiah and had great faith in Him, but he did not truly recognize Him as Jehovah God at this point.

He soon was to, however, when the Risen Christ appeared to all of the disciples and opened their eyes to His true identity. Philip is not mentioned again by name on the pages of the New Testament, but we can be sure that he continued to display zeal for missionary work and to win others for Christ just as he had done in the gospels.

B) NATHANAEL or BARTHOLOMEW

Bartholomew's name occurs in every list of the twelve, but other than this the New Testament remains silent. What little we can learn about this apostle is found in John's gospel under his forename of Nathanael. We have already noted that Bartholomew is not a first name, but rather a distinguishing second name. *Bar* means *son of*, and Bartholomew probably means *son of Tolmai.*

Our knowledge of Nathanael comes from two passages in the fourth gospel. He came from Cana in Galilee (John 21:2), and he was a friend of Philip (John 1:45). He seems to have been a skeptic at first not believing that anything good could come out of despised Nazareth, but he was won over by Philip's persistency and went to see for himself. It was not a wasted journey, for he was greeted with a wonderful testimony from the Master, "Here is a true Israelite in whom there is nothing false" (1:47, N.I.V.).

Nathanael was genuine when he believed that nothing good could come out of Nazareth, but he was soon put right, and he learned quickly. He was immediately impressed by the Lord's omniscience, and was quick to proclaim "Rabbi, thou art the Son of God; thou art the King of Israel" (1:49). With his heart now opened to recognize the Messiah, this pure, genuine Israelite was going to prove a faithful disciple in his service for the Lord, and he was promised a mighty reward for his belief (1:50-51).

C) MATTHEW

Matthew was the son of Alphaeus. His other name was Levi, and he was a tax collector by profession. This is all we really know about this disciple. His names are mentioned just eight times in the New Testament, and four of these are just the obligatory inclusion in the listings of the twelve.

The first time he appears on the scene is at his call (Matt. 9:9). Notice once again how immediate is the reaction of the person in response to the Lord's simple "Follow Me". We saw similar immediate allegiance from the fishing partners when they were called, and here again Matthew has no doubts that this Person had a special charisma about Him and an irresistible calling.

It must have been difficult for Peter, Andrew, James and John to leave their business, humanly speaking, to follow this new Prophet but it must have been doubly difficult for Matthew because he was employed by the ruling Roman authorities to collect taxes for them. The New Testament account seems to suggest that he just got up from his seat of custom, and followed Christ without notifying anyone. If this is the case, he would now become a wanted man for it was an offence to leave so important a post without notification.

In this sense he became an enemy of the Romans. Already he was an enemy of the Jews, for anyone who could abandon his countrymen and work for the alien Roman Empire, which oppressed the Israelites, was a despised man indeed. It would appear, then, that Matthew was a man of few friends although now he was to find a True Friend in Christ, and eleven new colleagues in the new vocation where he would lead people to find true friendship in the Lord.

Four of the New Testament references to Matthew deal with his call, the other four are merely a name-check in the listings. Of the first category, the accounts in Matt. 9:9 and Mark 2:14 are very brief and John does not mention the event at all. Luke is not exactly brimming over with information either, but at least he does informs us that Matthew owned his own house, and that after his call he prepared a great feast for the Lord (Luke 5:27-29). It appears that his house was not inconsiderable in size, reflecting his position in the service of the Romans and possibly his love of wealth, for it was certainly big enough to accommodate "a great company of publicans (tax-collectors) and of others".

Matthew, then, was a tax-collector and despised of the Jews. Publicans were regarded as the lowest of the low in their eyes and were linked with the other degenerate classes in the New

Testament such as harlots (Matt. 21:31-32), Gentiles (Matt. 18:7) and with sinners (Matt. 9:10-11; 11:19; Luke 7:34). Yet such is the wondrous way that God deals graciously with sinful human beings that Christ deliberately chose a collector of Roman taxes to become a collector of men for the Master.

A more unlikely candidate to be an apostle would be difficult to imagine, yet this type of person was the very type the Lord came to earth to redeem (Matt. 9:11-13). He linked Himself with people who needed His help. Mary Magdalene was demon-possessed (Luke 8:2); Simon was a zealot, perhaps little better than a bandit; Matthew was a tax-collector. To the Lord it made no difference what the outward appearance looked like, for He is no respecter of people and their worldly outlooks. He looks upon the heart, and He saw in Matthew a faithful servant whom He could use for His glory. So He did, and it is Matthew, of course, who was inspired by God to write the first book of our New Testament. He was the enemy who became a friend.

D) THOMAS

The most modern of all the twelve was Thomas, full of reservations and doubts, demanding proof, and commonly referred to as "Doubting Thomas". As is often the case, we have to look into John's gospel to find anything about this apostle, for the writer's of the synoptic gospels only mention his name.

Thomas was one of the twins, but we are never told who his other twin was. Thomas is the Hebrew, and Didymus (his other name) is the Greek for a twin (John 11:16). He first appears on the scene in this eleventh chapter of John in the account of the death of Lazarus. To go to Bethany, which was very close to Jerusalem, to raise His close friend Lazarus from the grave was a dangerous mission for the Lord, for His life was now in danger and there had already been two attempts to take it (John 8:59; 10:31). The disciples recognized this as a dangerous mission and tried to persuade Him not to undertake it (John 11:8), and only Thomas appears to speak up in favor of the trip. Not only does Thomas offer a voice of approval but he states that he is even willing to risk death, for if the Lord was to die he wanted to die with Him (11:16). Thomas, then, offers us a picture of a man of courage who would stand by his principles, and even die for them.

As we approach the last days of the Lord's life on earth, Thomas is recorded enquiring of Christ at the last supper. He seems to be a little confused by now, as were probably all of the disciples, for the Lord begins to talk of future homes in glory and Thomas does not understand. He does not doubt at this point, he just appears bewildered. It is Philip who displays unbelief here, not Thomas, and he is rebuked by the Lord for it (John 14:1-11).

After the resurrection the Lord made several appearances to His followers, and on one occasion He manifested Himself to the apostles while Thomas was not present. When told that the Risen Christ had appeared to them, he would not believe it and demanded proof for himself

(John 20:19-25). And so it was that eight days later Christ appeared to the apostolic band once again, and on this occasion He singled out Thomas for special attention. He answered Thomas' previous doubts by telling him to touch the wounds of His crucifixion, but the apostle has no need to do so as he submits to joyous worship by proclaiming "My Lord and my God" (verses 26-28), one of the greatest confessions of faith recorded in the New Testament.

Although he was mildly rebuked by the Lord because of his unbelief (John 20:29), Thomas learned his lesson and his faith would now be cemented because he made absolutely certain that the Lord had actually risen from the dead. There is every indication that Thomas became certain by doubting.

John offers us one further glimpse of Thomas in his gospel when he records the presence of the twin with the other disciples at another resurrection appearance by the sea of Tiberias (John 21:1-2). He realized he had missed out on real blessing by not being present at the first resurrection appearance, therefore there were to be no further miscalculations and he made sure he was present on this occasion. Perhaps his absence on the first occasion was not because of unbelief, we are not told. We are merely told that Thomas did not believe the other disciples when they informed him they had seen their Risen Master. Whatever the reason for his absence, there was certainly no doubts afterwards. He had learned his lesson and now wanted to be with the other believers, and to be numbered among those who were prepared to lay down their lives for their God and Saviour.

CHAPTER FIVE
THE FINAL GROUP

CHAPTER FIVE
THE FINAL GROUP

We have now considered eight of the apostles, split into two groups of four, and now we move on to the final group of four headed by James, the son of Alphaeus.

A) JAMES

These four disciples are generally considered to be the most insignificant amongst the apostolic group, not because of their lack of stature, for they were chosen of God to be His messengers, but because very little is actually recorded about them in the Scriptures. James, the son of Alphaeus certainly fits this bill, for the New Testament says absolutely nothing about him except his name in the four lists. James is the apostle about whom we know the least.

James is identified as the son of Alphaeus, which distinguished him from the other apostle James, the son of Zebedee. We also know from Scripture that Matthew was the son of Alphaeus (Mark 2:14), so there exists the possibility that these two disciples were brothers. The Bible does not tell us if it was the same Alphaeus who fathered both James and Matthew, and the fact that the New Testament never states that they were brothers nor includes them in the same grouping of four would provide negative evidence that they were not related. It is just a possibility.

The other speculations we can offer about James is that possibly he was a zealot, a Jewish nationalist. The linking of James, Thaddaeus, Simon and Judas together by the Holy Spirit is an indication that they had something in common, and the theme could be patriotism. Scripture informs us that Simon was a zealot. It is generally considered that Judas was one too, and there are some Latin manuscripts which include Thaddaeus as a member of the nationalist party. Nothing is said of James, the son of Alphaeus in this connection, but once again the hypothesis exists that he was a zealot and this is why the four are grouped together. Other than this we know nothing about James, the son of Alphaeus. Legend says that he preached in Persia and that he died a martyr by crucifixion, but this too is conjecture. He probably did die a martyr's death, however, for the common link amongst the apostles is that they were called by the Lord, they lived for His glory during their lives, and they all probably died for Him rather than renounce their faith.

B) THADDAEUS

Matthew calls this disciple "Lebbaeus, whose surname was Thaddaeus" (10:3 A.V.). Mark calls him just "Thaddeaus" (3:18); Luke describes him as "Judas the son of James" (Luke 6:16; Acts 1:13). Therefore we have Judas, Lebbaeus, Thaddaeus as our next disciple to consider.

In the first three gospels nothing is said of Thaddaeus other than the above references. As we have often seen, it is to John's gospel we have to go to piece our character descriptions together, but even then we only have one further reference to investigate. James, the son of Alphaeus is the apostle we know least about, but Thaddaeus is not far behind when it comes to New Testament information.

In John's gospel he makes one appearance under the name Judas, not Iscariot. At the last supper, he has one question to ask, "Lord how is it that Thou wilt manifest Thyself unto us, and not unto the world?" And the Lord replied, "If a man love Me, he will keep My words; and My Father will love him, and We will come unto him, and make Our abode with Him" (John 14:22-23).

If Judas, Lebbaeus, Thaddaeus was a zealot as we hinted at earlier in the chapter, this question was possibly prompted by his desire to see the Messiah manifesting Himself to the world in general, and the Romans in particular with outward pomp and glory. The Lord's answer put him right on this point, for His Kingdom was to be built on love and righteousness, not strength and power. It appears that Thaddaeus learned his lesson, for he is grouped together with the other disciples after the resurrection (Acts 1:13) in preparation to proclaim this kingdom of peace, whereas the other zealot, Judas, is not.

C) SIMON ZELOTES

The third obscure disciple of this final quartet is Simon the zealot, and once again the New Testament has nothing to add to his statutory inclusion in the four lists. You can see how difficult it is to work out a character study of these last three disciples, for if we remain within the confines of the New Testament, we have just one reference outside of the four lists and that is in John 14:22-23.

All we know for sure about Simon is that he was a zealot, and therefore a fervent nationalist who would detest the Roman powers that ruled in his beloved Palestine. This is fairly certain, for as we saw in the introduction, the Authorized Version rendering of "Simon the Canaanite" is wrong, and that the Revised Version, Revised Standard

Version and the New International Version have it correct as "Simon the Zealot".

Not only would a zealot hate a Roman, but he would also detest a Jew who associated himself with Rome. Therefore it is a remarkable situation that the constitution of the twelve included a Jewish patriot and a Jewish tax-collector who worked for the Romans. Such was the hatred that the zealots held for Roman sympathizers that it is not stretching a point too far to say that Simon probably would have attempted to kill Matthew had he met him under any other circumstances.

Here is one of the greatest of all examples of personal enmity destroyed by the common love of Christ. And Simon is still there after the Cross (Acts 1:13), offering us further proof that he had reconciled himself to the belief that the answer lay not in the sword, but rather in the love and truth of the Words of Christ. We can possibly sum Simon up best by stating that he was a man who began by hating but who ended up loving, transformed by the love of the Lord Jesus Christ.

D) JUDAS ISCARIOT

The fourth and final member of this probable group of zealots is the infamous Judas Iscariot. We have a lot to investigate regarding this controversial character, therefore we propose to devote the whole of the next chapter to this disciple who occupies the bottom place in the three lists of the disciples in the gospels, and who is omitted from the fourth list altogether - all for obvious reasons.

CHAPTER SIX

JUDAS ISCARIOT

CHAPTER SIX
JUDAS ISCARIOT

Judas Iscariot is an enigma. Chosen by God to be one of the twelve apostles, and to live on quite intimate terms with the Lord Jesus Christ for nearly three years, yet he failed miserably and concluded his life in suicidal shame. There are two schools of thought which prevail regarding Judas. The first, and most popular, version is that Judas was never a true believer in the first instance.

The second theory is that Judas recognized Jesus as the Messiah but failed to live up to expectations. As in the parable in Matthew 25:14-30, Judas became an unprofitable servant as opposed to the two servants who pleased their master by their good stewardships.

Before we consider these two options in detail, let us first of all consider the two references to

Judas in the New Testament outside of the passages dealing with his act of betrayal and suicide. They are both found in John's gospel.

After the feeding of the 5000, there was a movement to make Christ King by force (John 6:15), but when it became clear that the Lord's aims were different, many of his supporters drifted away and ceased to follow Him. The Lord asked His disciples if they wanted to forsake Him as well and it was Peter, as spokesman for the twelve, who strenuously protested their loyalty. The Master's reply was, "Have I not chosen you twelve, and one of you is a devil?" referring to Judas as the next verse informs us (John 6:66-71). Judas, who here is described as the son of Simon, was chosen by the Lord. Why did He choose one who was a devil?

The second incident involved the anointing of Christ with precious ointment by Mary of Bethany. Judas objected strongly; protesting that the money raised from the sale of the ointment could have been profitably used on the poor. The motive appears to be good, but notice what the

Holy Spirit says in the following verse, that he did it because he looked after the purse of the twelve and because he was a thief (John 12:1-8). Before we dismiss Judas out of hand, however, let us remember the words of the Lord, "He that is without sin among you, let him first cast a stone at her" (John 8:7).

The Lord said this in defense of a woman caught in adultery. He did not condemn her. He merely said, "sin no more" (v11). These profound words probably penetrated her heart to the extent that she became a changed woman, and who is to say that Judas remained a thief to the end of his days? We are just told that he was a thief at this point in time, which was fairly early in the Lord's ministry. And before we condemn the betrayer out of hand, let us ask ourselves, could we cast a stone at him? We accept salvation through the death and resurrection of the Lord Jesus Christ, and belief on His finished work on Calvary's Cross yet we still remain sinners, but sinners saved by grace. We still have our warts.

Peter was upbraided by Paul for prejudices against the Gentiles (Gal. 2:11-12); Paul argued with Barnabas so vehemently over Mark that they went on different missionary journeys (Acts 15:36-41); Demas forsook Paul altogether (2 Tim. 4:10); Timothy appears to have waivered (2 Tim. 1:5-8); Peter allowed Satan to influence him (Matt. 16:23); Thomas doubted (John 20:25); James and John wanted to bring fire down from heaven to destroy a village and its inhabitants (Luke 9:54); Nathanael was contemptuous of the Nazarines (John 1:46); Philip was doubtful about taking non-Jews to the Lord (John 12:20-22). It is the same with such Old Testament characters as Moses, David and Abraham who committed murder, adultery and who lied respectively. The list is almost endless. These were all saved men who still made major mistakes in their lives. Is it not possible that Judas came into this category?

It was in the closing days of our Lord's earthly life that Judas played a leading role in the proceedings. The problem of the Jewish authorities was how to get Christ into their hands without causing a riot, for He was still popular with the common people. It was Judas who solved their problem for them, for we are told that Satan entered into him (Luke 22:3), and he betrayed the Lord for thirty pieces of silver.

Scripture informs us that Satan entered Judas at this point. Therefore whatever he was before, he was certainly not demon-possessed. Had he been so, the Lord would have exorcised him for there was to be no Satanic influence on the ministry of the twelve as they proclaimed the good news of the forthcoming Kingdom. Let us not under-estimate the powers of the devil. Scripture describes him as "fallen from heaven, O Lucifer, son of the morning" (Isa. 14:12); "perfect in beauty", "the anointed cherub", "perfect in thy ways" (Ezek. 28:12-15); and he has the ability to enter God's presence as the Lord permits (Job 1:6; 2:1).

In the New Testament the fallen one is given such impressive titles as "the prince of the power of the air" (Eph. 2:2); "the god of this world" (2 Cor. 4:4; John 12:31); and it also informs us that he can transform himself into an angel of light in order to deceive God's elect (2 Cor. 11:4). This is illustrated vividly in the cases of Eve (1 Tim. 22:14); Ananias and Sapphira (Acts 5:3); and Peter (Matt. 16:23). Did Satan deceive Judas in a similar manner? Notice how Ananias and Sapphira lost their human lives, but did they lose their eternal life in glory? If they were true believers, as the context appears to indicate, it was impossible for them to lose their salvation because God cannot go back on His Word (Num. 23:19; Mal. 3:6; Heb. 6:17); it is impossible for Him to lie (Titus 1:2; Heb. 6:18); and no one, not even Satan, is able to pluck a believer out of the hand of the Lord (John 10:28).

The gospel accounts of Judas' act of betrayal are well known (Matt. 26:14-16 and 47-50; Mark 14:10-21 and 43-46; Luke 22:3-23 and 47-48; John 13:18-30 and 18:1-5). What is interesting to note is that Matthew and Mark are both constrained by the Holy Spirit to use the word *kataphilein* for Judas kiss of betrayal, which means "to kiss thoroughly, to be very friendly" (Young's Concordance). This word is used on only four other occasions in the New Testament and a study of the four passages clearly indicates a kissing embrace, and act of love, not merely a sign of salutation or identification (Luke 7:38; 7:45; 15:20; Acts 20:37). This does not prove that Judas believed that Jesus was the Messiah, but obviously he held the Lord in high esteem and had become greatly attached to Him.

Judas, then, betrays his Master with one final embrace of love and affection, not hatred and detestation, and almost immediately he is full of remorse when he realizes he has committed a dreadful deed. He returns to the chief priests and elders, informs them he has sinned against innocent blood, is rebuffed, throws away the blood money and goes and hangs himself (Matt. 27:3-5). The account in Acts informs us that Judas "burst asunder in the midst, and all his bowels gushed out" (Acts 1:16-19). This is not a contradiction, for anyone left hanging from a tree for a considerable period of time would experience the stretching of the body, resulting in gross swelling which could then cause bursting.

Piecing these two accounts together, let us note what the Holy Spirit has to say of Judas. "He repented himself" (Matt. 27:3); "I have sinned" (27:4); "I have betrayed innocent blood" (27:4); "He hanged himself" (27:5); "He was numbered with us (the disciples)" (Acts 1:17); "He obtained part of this ministry" (1:17); his was "the reward of iniquity" (1:18); "his bishopric let another take" (1:20).

Judas recognized he had sinned, and he repented. The Greek word here is *metanelomai* which is not the strongest Greek word for repent. The usual word is *metanoeo,* and perhaps a better translation would be "regretted". The New International Version is near the mark with "seized with remorse". We cannot say that Judas definitely repented of his sin and turned to God for deliverance, but on the other hand he was certainly full of remorse for his actions and he regretted betraying his Master. He recognized that he had sinned and that he had betrayed innocent blood, and he appears to be just a step away from true repentance. Perhaps he did repent, we are not told, for the next fact we are told is that Judas went and hung himself. This appears to be the sign of a defeated man.

"He was numbered with us, and had obtained part of this ministry" (Acts 1:17) is a statement which provokes two schools of thought. Those who believe that Judas was not a true believer in the first instance state that he was allocated a place amongst the twelve which he subsequently lost, and that this verse is not referring to any eternal consequences.

Those who believe that Judas was a deceived believer, however, claim that this verse does have eternal considerations. The reasoning is that his place amongst the twelve included the prize of sitting on the twelve thrones in the coming kingdom, a prize which he forfeited. His reward was lost but not his salvation. This would seem to be confirmed by Acts 1:20, "his bishopric let another take". Matthias took the place of Judas amongst the twelve, but not his place in glory for he had a place of his own already. Judas suffered "the reward of iniquity".

This applies to us as well. We have our stewardship to work out, or as Paul puts it, "good works, which God hath before ordained that we should walk in them" (Eph. 2:10). If we fail, we lose out on rewards in glory but not salvation; "if any man's work shall be burned, he shall suffer loss, but he himself shall be saved, yet so by fire" (1 Cor. 3:15). This could supply the answer to the difficult saying of the Lord referring to Judas, "woe unto that man by whom the Son of Man is betrayed. It had been good for that man if he had not been born" (Matt. 26:24). Surely the Lord is here referring to Judas' gruesome death, for there is no mention of judgment of any suffering in eternity. Once again opinions are divided on this problematic position of Judas – unbelieving disciple or misguided believer.

Judas is called "the son of perdition" (John 17:12), and much is read into this. The word in Greek is *apoleia* which does not always carry such a strong translation. It is rendered "waste" in Matt. 26:8 and Mark 14:4 regarding the wasted oil and either "lose" or "lost" in the accounts of the lost sheep, lost coin and lost son (Luke 15:4-

32), and lost sheep (Matt. 10:6; 15:24). It could well be that Judas was the disciple who *wasted* his vocation and who *lost* his bishopric, and with it one of the greatest treasures in the New Testament.

We have to decide, however, what was lost? Salvation cannot be lost, therefore it cannot refer to this. It could refer to Judas himself who was possibly not a saved person in the first instance, or it could refer to his position of authority as a reward in glory. In the accounts of the lost sheep, coin and son it is the article which is deemed to have perished, not the person who lost the item in question. He just suffered a loss. An example of this is the prodigal son who was lost (perished, suffered perdition), but when found was deemed to have risen from the dead (Luke 15:24). The father suffered loss, but it was the son who was actually lost. The parallel would appear to be that Judas suffered loss, but it was the bishopric or prize which was lost to him. In all three cases the sheep, the coin and the son were found again. If it was Judas who was lost, how could he be found again? He was either saved or he was not.

He cannot be saved one moment and lost the next.

Perhaps the verses that give most conviction to the case for the loss of Judas himself are found in John 13:10-11, "He that is washed needeth not save to wash his feet, but is clean every whit: and ye are clean, but not all. For He knew who should betray Him; therefore said He, 'Ye are not all clean'". The distinction usually drawn from this passage is that he who has been cleaned (bathed) once for all by Christ's blood needs only the day to day contaminations, caused by a walk in the world, washed off, hence the bathing of feet. The contention is that Judas did not have this once for all "baptism", even though he might have been baptized in water. This is a very strong case.

It is always dangerous to build concrete ideas on one passage, however, and there is certainly enough doubts over some of the other Scripture to leave an open mind on the eternal standing of the betrayer. Even this last reference in John can be interpreted to refer to reward. The prize is awarded for continual good stewardship, hence the need for a daily appraisal of our service and our standing before the Lord. Those who go on to maturity and perfection receive the crown (2 Tim. 2:11-13; 4:6-8). Judas did not. The other eleven disciples did.

Judas, then, is a real enigma to us. Granted some of the greatest privileges bestowed upon New Testament servants of God, he failed miserably and ended in shame. He was chosen by the Lord, chosen to serve Him not to betray Him. Judas had a free will and chose his own slippery path. Chosen by God, then, there must have been a great deal in the character of Judas to commend him. He was granted the honor of living on quite intimate terms with Christ for the best part of three years and became very attached to Him as is demonstrated in his loving kiss and embrace on their final meeting. He recognized his great mistake realizing he had betrayed innocent blood, and he was full of remorse at his deed. At this point he was very near to true repentance, but here the issue becomes debatable. Did Judas truly repent? We are not told. His following act of suicide might suggest he did not.

Scripture has much to say about Judas which is far from derogatory. On the other hand, however, it does also contain much which is far from complimentary. He is called a thief, a devil, the son of perdition. His was the reward of iniquity, he lost his bishopric, he was "unclean" and the Lord stated that it would have been better for Judas if he had not been born. Very strong words, and perhaps the case for the betrayer being an unbeliever carries more conviction than the one for him being a deluded, deceived believer in the Lord Jesus Christ.

Let us not judge, however, (Matt. 7:1-2) for we certainly cannot cast stones. David committed adultery and murder; Samson broke his Nazarite vow; Abraham lied about his wife Sarah on two occasions; Moses killed and Egyptian on one occasion and disobeyed God on another; Jacob was continually found cheating hence his name means "supplanter". Yet all of these people were not just believers, but Hebrews chapter eleven includes every one of these in the examples of God's servants who exhibited great faith! We are all sinners who fall short of the glory of God, even when saved by His wondrous grace, for He still loves a penitent heart. Did Judas repent in his heart? Matthew 27:3 offers the possibility. "Then Judas, which had betrayed Him, when he saw that he was condemned, repented himself, and brought again the thirty pieces of silver to the chief priests and elders". It could well be that the valuable possession which Judas forfeited was the crown of sitting on one of the twelve thrones judging the nation of Israel. He certainly lost this. Did he lose anything else? Let us leave it with the Perfect Righteous Judge. We make mistakes in our judgment. He does not.

CHAPTER

SEVEN

MATTHIAS

CHAPTER SEVEN
MATTHIAS

The thirteenth disciple we have to consider is Judas' replacement, Matthias. Not a great deal is known about him, but he has a significant role to play in the future government of the nation of Israel, for as we have seen, he has a key part to play in judging the twelve tribes.

Some might object to a fairly obscure figure such as Matthias taking over the bishopric of Judas, when there were far more notable contenders such as Luke, Paul, Barnabas, James the Lord's brother or even Timothy. After all Matthias is never mentioned in the four gospels, and for that matter he is never mentioned again by name in the New Testament after his appointing as a disciple in Acts 1:23-26. These great men of God all had their parts to play in the plan and purposes of the Almighty, but were they really candidates for the vacant position in the apostolic team? The answer is an emphatic "No"!

There were certain qualification for a man to join this elite company of God's servants, and they are enumerated for us in Scripture. The new apostle had to be a man who was with the Lord Jesus and the other eleven at the beginning of His ministry, at His baptism in the river Jordan by John the Baptist through to the Lord's death, resurrection and ascension (Acts 1:21-22; John 15:27).

Only two men seem to have fitted these requirements perfectly, namely Matthias and another follower, Joseph called Barsabas, who was surnamed Justus (1:23). He, like Matthias, is never mentioned again on the pages of the New Testament. However, other candidates could not match these two for these necessary qualifications, for none of them had witnessed the appropriate events. In addition to this, Luke was a Gentile, which would rule him out, for the replacement needed to be a Jew, to be a minister to the circumcision group. Luke also holds the distinction of being the only Gentile to be selected by God to write two books of the Bible, for the other sixty four books are all written by Jews. The Apostle Paul was chosen to be the "Apostle to the Gentiles" (2 Tim. 1:11; Eph. 3:1; Gal. 2:2-9), and followers such as Barnabas, Timothy, Titus and John Mark were all appointed to help him in his work amongst the Gentiles. The ministry of the twelve was clearly to be to the nation of Israel (Matt. 10:5-6; Gal. 2:7-9; James 1:1).

Returning to the account in Acts, we notice that the group of believers prayed to the Lord for guidance in appointing the new apostle, the lot fell upon Matthias and he was numbered with the other apostles (1:24-26). This was not a lottery as we might think in our modern world, but rather this was God's appointed method of divine guidance frequently used in Old Testament times, (e.g. Lev. 16:8-10; Num. 26:55-56; Josh. 18:6-11; Neh. 10:34).

There is absolutely no doubt here that Matthias was the choice of the Lord, and that Joseph was not rejected on the grounds of chance or luck. The lot which fell upon Matthias was God's lot. This was confirmed by the tongues of fire on Matthias at Pentecost as well as upon the other eleven (Acts 2:1-3).

This is all we know of the new disciple. He was a follower of Christ right from the Lord's baptism, always around playing a quiet role in the background, yet ever faithful even though through the difficult periods. And he was still loyal after the crucifixion for he is found with the other believers in the opening chapter of the Acts (compare verses 21, 22 with verses 3, 6, 9-14). And no doubt he was faithful unto death, for he was to be a witness in "Jerusalem, and to all Judea, and in Samaria, and unto the uttermost part of the earth" (1:8). And of course, he took the place of Judas and will inherit the prize or crown of sitting on one of the twelve thrones to judge the twelve tribes of Israel (Matt. 19:28; Luke 22:30; Rev. 21:12-14).

SUMMARY

SUMMARY

What can we conclude about these thirteen chosen men of God? They were all probably faithful unto death, with the exception of Judas, although the New Testament only records the martyrdom of James (Acts 12:1-2).

The inner circle of three were regarded as the leaders of the apostolic band, with Peter being the spokesman. His brother Andrew must have been on the fringe of this leading trio, and like them was a partner in the fishing business. All four became fishers of men.

Philip was the loyal disciple who disliked responsibility, but who displayed great missionary tendencies. Nathanael was the pure, genuine Israelite who learned quickly that contempt was a sin. Matthew was the collector of taxes who became the collector of men's hearts. Thomas was the apostle who became certain by doubting. We know so little about James, the son of Alphaeus, Thaddaeus and Simon the Zealot, the three who appear almost insignificant on the pages of the New Testament.

What we can be sure of is that they were not insignificant in the eyes of the Lord. If they were zealous nationalists before, they became zealous missionaries afterwards in the service of their Risen Master.

What can we add about Judas? He missed out on so much that the Lord had in store for him. He committed one of the greatest sins in the history of the world, and lost his appointed place in the Kingdom. Yet there remains the possibility that he himself was not lost, but rather his position of leadership. His place, of course, was taken by Matthias another disciple we know so little about. He, in fact, is one of four disciples who is mentioned only by name in the New Testament.

The final twelve all witnessed the small beginnings, some of them responded to a simple "Follow Me". They progressed to the Lord's baptism, to His numerous miracles and to His wonderful teaching. Three of them were privileged to see His transfiguration in glory and to be with the Lord during His final agony in the Garden of Gethsemane. Peter was bold enough to be in a position to fail by being the only apostle to follow the Lord after His arrest even though this led to his denials.

Finally they all witnessed the Messiah in Resurrection glory, and were privileged to see His glorious ascension from earth to the heavenly places. This must have greatly encouraged them and given them new heart to take the message of Christ to Jerusalem, to Judea, to Samaria and beyond. Some met violent deaths.

Some suffered tremendous persecution and physical hardship. But they never flinched in their resolve once they had been stimulated by their Risen Lord, and these twelve great men of God will undoubtedly hear the words of the Master, "Well done thou good and faithful servant … I will make thee ruler over many things; enter thou into the joy of the Lord" (Matt. 25:21), before He grants them their crowning positions in glory upon the twelve majestic thrones in the nation of Israel.

BOOKS ON PRAYER

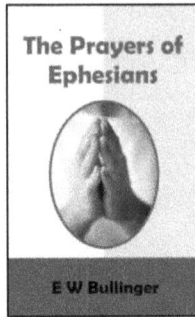

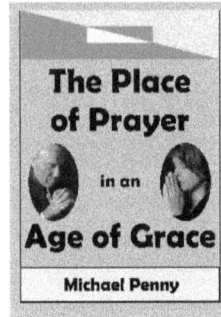

Unanswered Prayer
Neville Stephens

The Prayers of Ephesians
E W Bullinger

The Place of Prayer in an Age of Grace
Michael Penny

Prayer that is … Powerful and Effective
Andrew Morton

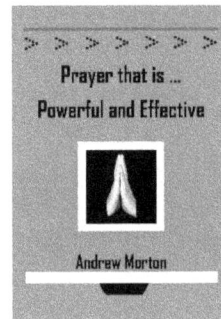

Further details of these books can be seen on www.obt.org.uk

They can be ordered from that website.

They are available as eBooks from
Amazon and Apple and also as
KDP paperbacks from Amazon.

FURTHER READING

Approaching the Bible

Michael Penny

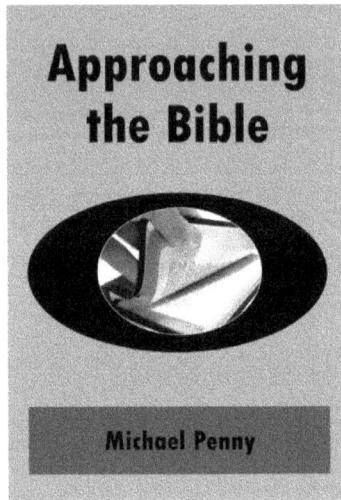

If you have enjoyed reading this publication on prayer you will find *Approaching the Bible* helpful and interesting. In an easy to read style and with an easy to understand method, it does an excellent job of following the advice of Bishop Miles Coverdale, which was contained in the first Bible printed in English. That advice was based on asking such questions as:

- "Who" were these words written to, or

"Who" were they about?
- "Where" is this to take place?
- "When" was it written or "When" is it about?
- "What", precisely, is said?
- "Why" did God say it, do it, or will do it?

After asking such questions, we then will have a better understanding of the passage we are considering and can better apply it to our lives today.

Further details of this book can be seen on www.obt.org.uk

It can be ordered from that website.

It is available as an eBook from Amazon and Apple and also as KDP paperbacks from Amazon.

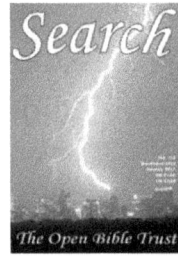

ABOUT THIS BOOK

The Twelve Disciples

The Twelve Disciples are the most talked about group of people in Christian circles but who can name all twelve? Not only that, but how much do we know about these men?

In this publication Neville Stephens searches the Scriptures and draws together **all** that the Bible has to say on these men.

He makes a number of interesting comments on both Judas and his replacement, Matthias, and *The Twelve Disciples* actually deals with thirteen.

Publications of The Open Bible Trust must be in accordance with its evangelical, fundamental and dispensational basis. However, beyond this minimum, writers are free to express whatever beliefs they may have as their own understanding, provided that the aim in so doing is to further the object of The Open Bible Trust. A copy of the doctrinal basis is available at

www.obt.org.uk/doctrinal-basis

or from:

THE OPEN BIBLE TRUST
Fordland Mount, Upper Basildon,
Reading, RG8 8LU, UK.

www.ingramcontent.com/pod-product-compliance
Lightning Source LLC
Chambersburg PA
CBHW070533030426
42337CB00016B/2191